OLD RICHMOND

ALFRED STIRLING

MELBOURNE
THE HAWTHORN PRESS

First published 1979
© Alfred Stirling
ISBN 0 7256 0251 1

*Wholly set up and printed in Australia by
The Hawthorn Press Pty Ltd
601 Little Bourke Street, Melbourne 3000*

*This book, part of which is based on an address
delivered to The Royal Historical Society of
Victoria on Tuesday evening, 1 May 1979, is
limited to an edition of 1000 copies and printed by
The Hawthorn Press*

Contents

Old Richmond

Richmond, 'old Richmond', is a word that, even more than the name of its neighbour Jolimont, suggests a beautiful green-treed mountain or hillside, the original Richmond being in Brittany. It still has a slightly romantic ring to it. To some Australians perhaps it conjures up the old townships of the late eighteenth century near Sydney and Hobart with their rivers and Georgian bridges and hillside churches.

To others it means the Thames in Surrey with Richmond Hill and the 'Star and Garter' and long summer evenings by the river; or even perhaps a northern Richmond with its castle on the Swale, in Yorkshire.

The Richmond of Surrey owes its name to Henry VII, whose former title was Earl of Richmond.

To Americans it recalls the stately old Virginian city beside 'the mighty James', the capital of the Confederacy for five years, and the centre of a long struggle. They tell the story still of an old-time black porter at Washington's Union Station who, when asked by a passenger how long it took to get to Richmond, replied, 'They do say it took Gen'l Grant five years'. Shakespeare rightly said, in the context of the Wars of the Roses: 'I think there be six Richmonds in the field.'

It is rather surprising that after nearly a century and a half there have been few books on Victoria's Richmond. Other suburbs have done better: Brighton, with Professor Weston Bate's classic, comes first to mind. There have long been books on Prahran, Kew, Caulfield and, more lately, Heidelberg, Blackburn, Nunawading, and many others.

Richmond, of course, gets mention in most of the early chronicles of Melbourne, but often only fleetingly. One exception is Agnes Paton Bell's *Melbourne: John Batman's Village,* which carries well into the recent mid-century and often looks at Richmond. Her first pen-picture is of

> the Yarra Flat two miles east of Melbourne where timber cutters felled the gum trees and floated them downstream. Richmond Hill, sloping up from the Yarra, was so named because it reminded Englishmen of Richmond on the Thames (and the area beyond the river to the east was at the same time called Kew). During the year in which Melbourne was named, the Chief Surveyor, Robert Hoddle, mapped out these new places. The plan shows Richmond Road (Bridge Road) running along the ridge of the hill, with the Richmond blocks of land of 25 to 28 acres each. Quarries of bluestone were opened up and it too was floated downstream, in barges.

'Garryowen' (Edmund Finn of *The Herald* and *The Chronicles of Early Melbourne* (1888)) told of 'the green, undulating, well-timbered bush of Richmond', while William Westgarth, MLC, a Scot who 'went home' after seventeen years of public service in Victoria, described his 'first day in Melbourne', in 1840, when he was twenty-five, in his '50 years after' memoirs:

> I had engaged to accompany a young friend that evening to spend the next day, Sunday, at his 'country seat' on Richmond Flat, where he had constructed, mostly with his own hands, a sort of hut or wigwam, under

an unchallenged squattage. We wandered about in the pouring rain for the rest of the night. . . . A beauteous sunny morning broke upon us, near the Yarra. Solitude and quiet reigned around us, excepting the enchanging 'ting-tong' of the bell-birds.

However, Westgarth did not follow his friend's example and instead of Richmond's Yarra he set himself up on the banks of the Merri Creek, where he is now commemorated in the northern suburb, Westgarth. He kept close links with Richmond. Professor Geoffrey Serle has portrayed Westgarth clearly in *The Golden Age*. He originally came from Edinburgh where his father was Surveyor-General of Customs. A member of the first Council of Victoria, the leader of Melbourne's mercantile community, he was 'affable, modest, urbane — and above all tolerant . . . the complete democrat'.

The first land sales were in 1837 (and these were followed in 1839 and 1848). There were forty-seven blocks. The first purchasers included the Reverend Joseph Docker, Dr Farquhar McCrae, William Highett, John Muston, and later W. B. Burnley (MLC in the first Legislature and a pioneer councillor of Richmond) and Nathaniel Guthridge. At least three of these men played a part in Richmond's early history. Guthridge, however, soon moved on to pioneer Gippsland, becoming first Mayor of Sale and a Member of Parliament, and running a line of steamers from the Gippsland Lakes (Red Bluff) to Port Phillip until his death in 1878. Other early purchasers were Captains Octavius Burton and Septimus Martin. Richmond got its full share of youngest sons of the large families of the Victorian era.

Dr McCrae, who flits through the Journals of his brother's

wife Georgiana, sold his block after ten years for £200. He died in 1851.

JOSEPH DOCKER : ST STEPHENS

Joseph Docker is the first of the few big names to emerge from Richmond's early story. There are only a handful of them. He was a clergyman from the far north of England, Westmoreland (now merged in Cumbria), of an old-established family of farmers, armigerous, and fiercely independent. As a young graduate of Oxford, he had gone to Sydney in the late 1820s as a colonial chaplain and held the parish of Windsor, with St Matthew's, one of Greenway's most beautiful churches. The love of the land was strong in his blood and he took up a sheep-run there called Clifton, perhaps after the early ship of that name. He not only did good — he did well. The legend that he was defrocked by the bishop was quite false; but after a few years at Windsor he fell out with his peppery bishop, whose chief complaint was that the rector spent too much time on the farm, and in 1839 he overlanded to Victoria. He at once bought about sixty acres of the Richmond Hill for £48 and he named it the Clifton Estate. He would have liked the 'township', then a mere hamlet, to be called Clifton.

Twenty years later, in the late 'sixties, he sold it all, sub-dividing it into lots of eight to twenty-five acres. At its zenith, Docker's land stretched from Punt Road to Church Street and from Swan Street to Richmond Terrace. He gave the Church of England a large and splendid site on the south-eastern corner of Richmond Hill, this part being long called Docker's Hill. On this, in 1851, was built St Stephen's, one of the finest churches in Melbourne, a huge church of bluestone with four aisles and originally two galleries, and now still standing in a grove of century-old oaks and elms.

Docker also built a house for himself close to the church, a pleasant house of simple lines, with wrought-iron balconies and slender verandah columns, a 'double' house, which he called 'Clifton House'. Later my grandparents bought it and simplified it by dropping the rather grandiose suffix and calling it 'Clifton'. After my grandfather's early death, my grandmother retained half, and her eldest son and his young family lived in the other half, renaming the sister-house 'Sorella'. 'Clifton' has now been demolished, but it survives in a fine photograph in the book *Early Melbourne Architecture* which Lady Casey and a group of architects, lawyers and other friends produced about twenty-five years ago.

Docker had lived in one half of the house and installed his Melbourne agent in the other. He also built a seaside house on land bought from J. G. Vautier, standing in Vautier Street, Elwood, still called 'Elwood House', the oldest in that district. It, too, has been in its long life both a double and a single house. However, Docker only used the Richmond and Elwood houses as his *pied à terre*. His real domain was Wangaratta, dating from his overland trek. There he had acquired a very large estate and in 1858 built a splendid towered Italianate palazzo, 'Bontherambo', which his family occupy to this day.

In Parson Docker's favour it should be recalled that his benevolence included a rare understanding of how to deal with the aborigines of North-Eastern Victoria.

When he subdivided 'Docker's Hill' the new streets intersecting it were called Docker, Clifton and Bontherambo, now spelled Botherambo. (Mr Standish Keon, long linked with Richmond, tells me the change to 'bother' came from schoolboys, hurrying up the hill to school; a fine instance of popular etymology.)

Docker had initially thought to graze sheep on his Clifton Estate. He certainly planted a large orchard there, but his manager neglected it. Miss Mary Turner Shaw, who with her tongue and pen has recreated in true Turner colour the dawn of the sheep industry in Western Victoria, and also the sunset days of famous city theatres, has provided for us a 'Docker' indenture of over a century ago. The land, in Clifton Street, passed through the hands of two Shaw brothers, Jonathan, of Richmond, and Thomas the Younger, of Wooriwyrite, known, as was his father, Thomas Shaw, not only as a pioneer breeder of merino sheep but a highly articulate exponent of causes such as temperance.

I have a memory of one of Joseph Docker's sons, from when I was about eight, which came back as I watched the third Test match at the Melbourne Cricket Ground at New Year. I thought back to the first Australia-England Test match I had seen and how, having strayed from my parents, probably with autograph book in hand, I was sitting in front of the pavilion and had one of my first conversations with an adult on a man-to-man basis. A very old man, immensely tall with a white beard and benevolent expression, was sitting just in front of me. He turned around, greeted me, introduced himself, and I am relieved to recall that without prompting I gave my name. For at once he said, 'I remember your father hitting a ball about when he was about your age and we were living in Church Street, Richmond', and he told me to be sure to give my father his regards. He told me that he lived near Wangaratta and had come to town especially for the cricket, and we swapped views, considerably building up my self-confidence. 'Parson

Docker' was never vicar of St Stephen's, though he did so much to establish it.

St Stephen's first incumbent, Canon Perks, a Shropshire man, then twenty-five, from London University, filled the post for nearly half a century. His interminable sermons helped to empty the church. Mrs Perks's attempts to check his garrulity were well known. She sat in the front pew below the pulpit and when she had had enough she pulled a large watch from her reticule and swung it to and fro. If this failed, which it rarely did, she dropped her hymn book on the floor with a loud thud. Only once, when this dread thunder failed, did Mrs Perks have to resort to extreme measures. She rose and stumped down the long aisle, leaving the Canon speechless. At the turn of the century Canon Perks died and was succeeded by the Reverend Arthur Tress, who gave shorter sermons. Later came the Reverend L. L. Wenzel, whose widow was an active member of the Richmond and Burnley Historical Society up to the last week of her long life of over ninety years, dying in mid-1979. Her father, the builder Clements Langford, did much for St Stephen's and even more for the completion of the spires of St Paul's Cathedral.

THE GROWTH OF THE CITY

Richmond was separated from Melbourne in 1855, but it was not created a town until 1872. In 1882, after very rapid growth, it was made a city. In 1894, despite the crash, it 'went electric light', one of the first to do so.

The first Melbourne Directory I have seen which 'specifies' Richmond is that of 1860. It defines a sprawling quadrilateral: on the north Victoria Parade, on the south and the east the River Yarra, and on the west Punt Road. Across this stretched the ridge of tall hills from what was already East Melbourne to what became Burnley.

The main streets were Bridge Road, from east to west; Church Street, crossing it, from north to south, with the curving river at both of its ends, thus half-encircling Richmond on the south, east and north; River Bank; and Swan Street and Highett Street, two narrower streets running parallel with Bridge Road. Other streets from north to south were Lennox, Union, Rotherwood, and from east to west Cremorne Street, a name soon to become famous.

Punt Road faced west across almost open country — the huge police paddock where soon the Richmond and Melbourne Cricket and Football Clubs (Richmond Tigers) were to arise and the whole area to be glamourised as Yarra Park. Just beyond this lay the little garden suburb of Jolimont on its hill, site of the first Government House under Charles La Trobe and his Swiss wife. Jolimont was strictly an extension of East Melbourne, but early Richmond liked to claim it as a small satellite. Soon it acquired its own Member of Parliament.

In the first few years of Richmond the approach from Melbourne was regarded as dangerous. In the area, still heavily timbered, known as Fitzroy Square, bushrangers lurked and held up travellers along Richmond Road. Until the 1860s it was probably safer to travel to Richmond by the *Pride of the Yarra*, or the iron *Export*. The steamer left Prince's Bridge every hour from 9 am till 6 pm, with four stops: the Botanic Gardens, Punt Road, the Tannery and Church Street Bridge. The fare was sixpence each way.

In 1855 James Sinclair, a landscape gardener, came to Melbourne from Russia, where he had — until the outbreak of the Crimean War — been laying out the gardens of Prince Woronzoff's villa in the Crimea (destined to be Churchill's headquarters at the fateful Yalta Conference of 1945). In 1862 he transformed Fitzroy Square into the sixty-four acres of Fitzroy Gardens, with their avenues of 120-year-old elms.

Four-horse omnibuses and later trams came, and then in the 1880s the dark-blue cable-trams. The railway from Melbourne to Richmond was built in 1859, across the low area between Richmond Hill and the river. It ran every half-hour between Melbourne and Richmond Station at Punt Road.

In the same year, Richmond also got, for a few short years, its daily newspaper, the *Australian*. A leading article of 1860 points out that Richmond had not yet been proclaimed a city, in line with its northern neighbour Fitzroy. Richmond, it said, had been 'wholly intended for farming and grazing'. It had 'not become a business offshoot of Melbourne, but a residential one'. It was described as being 'a beautiful extensive slope, on both sides' and 'very salubrious'.

But as early as 1851 it had acquired 2000 houses for its 9000 people. By 1861 the population was 12,000; the total for Melbourne was 126,000. The gold rush was on, affecting all Melbourne. 'Garryowen' wrote of Richmond's retention of a country atmosphere — *'rus in urbe* boxes for business and professional men'. He pointed out that these villas were comfortable but 'never grandiose, as in other suburbs'. He instanced W. B. Burnley, 'a very rich man' from Yorkshire, whose subdivisions led to the eastern flats being given his name; and Judge Robert Pohlman, one of the first batch of barristers to arrive from England (actually he was from Scotland, and thus an 'advocate'). Pohlman arrived in 1840, still in his early twenties, and with a still younger brother. Together they took up a station curiously named 'Elephant Bridge' at Darlington (called after nearby Mt Elephant). But within two years he had turned to law, for which he had been trained, and was quickly admitted to the Victorian Bar. Pohlman long remained faithful to Punt Road, close to the Bridge Road corner, even after it ceased to be all-residential, and some pubs and shops took over. Then there was George Cavenagh, a young Irishman, of an old family of Wexford, the founder of the original Melbourne *Herald*. Cavenagh, wrongly described as an 'emancipist', came over from New South Wales, where he had been the second editor of the *Sydney Gazette,* originally an official newspaper founded by Governor King in 1803. In Sydney, Cavenagh had to fight almost monthly libel actions; in Melbourne, we read, he was thrashed in public three times by his victims. I doubt this, although he was involved in one near-duel. Some of the early chroniclers speak of Cavenagh more admiringly. Certainly he founded the MCC and was its president for seven years. He was a very early member of the Melbourne Club, although not a founder member.

Before long another Irishman, Samuel Winter, a very distinguished editor, bought the *Herald* from Cavenagh. Cavenagh lived for some years in Flinders Lane but later returned to Richmond, living on Lennox Street Hill.

Mrs Agnes Paton Bell enlarges 'Garryowen's' picture considerably when she tells of the rise of big business in Melbourne around 1850: 'Commercial men who dealt with banking, exchange trade and insurance: they formed the Chamber of Commerce' (William Westgarth being the prime mover). Many of these wealthy men, she tells us, moved away from Eastern Hill at the gates of the city to build big houses with rooms thirty by twenty feet for themselves, in parklands, in the villages of Brighton and Hawthorn, 'houses which astounded visitors from London'.

As they moved away, successful professional men, lawyers, doctors, bankers and city business-members of country landowning-families took their places in the 2 or 3 storeyed town houses of Collins Street, Spring Street and Flinders Street. . . . Professional and businessmen who wanted one or two horses, a big garden, their own cows and pigs, moved out to Richmond Hill, the coming fashionable district, where the original 25 acre blocks were being divided into 6 acre blocks, the remaining area being used for 'streets broad and narrow'. . . . On the north side, the sunny side, looking towards the blue sweep of the Plenty Range, the Chief Surveyor (Robert Hoddle), a leading chemist (Joseph Bosisto) and a banker (William Highett) built big homes. . . . On the south side, looking over the Yarra, a member of the pioneer Henty family bought one of the big blocks — in 1851 — and a leading doctor, Thomas Black, built the spacious mansion of 'Pine Grove' wherein many important affairs of the City were decided at his select dinner parties.

Georgiana McCrae in her diaries recorded visits to and from Dr Black and his daughter.

Like Mrs McCrae, Dr Black was a Scot. He was very concerned to have an Australian bank in Melbourne to balance the two English banks, and to this end enlisted the support of Henry Miller, the first Mayor of Richmond, and a millionaire. Miller came from Londonderry, the son of a

Peninsular War officer who was an early commandant in Van Diemen's Land. For a time Henry Miller, 'methodical, homely and unobtrusive', was Minister of Customs. The Bank of Victoria was his monument, and it was virtually founded in Dr Black's dining room at 'Pine Grove' in 1862. The splendid Italianate façade and domed chamber in central Collins Street were ruthlessly demolished a few years ago.

Miller did not live in Richmond for long. His first house, built in 1850, was a large wooden one in Bridge Road, opposite the Town Hall. He soon moved to 'Findon', a new mansion in Kew, with thirty acres, high above the Yarra. When he died, Miller's estate was sworn at £1,500,000. He left about fifty grandchildren. Members of his family sat on the board of the Bank of Victoria for over a century and many of them gave generous public service to the State.

There was a direct communication between Richmond and the south side of Melbourne (South Yarra) by two punts, the first established in 1842 at the east end of Bridge Road, opposite St James's Park in Hawthorn, later replaced in 1855 by a wooden bridge and in 1858 by an iron bridge. Another punt followed in 1852, at Punt Road, which continued up the hill across the river. The view up Punt Hill was very pleasant, the whole of one side being a vineyard. 'Fairlie House', owned by the pioneer Col. Joseph Anderson, stretched west to the Botanic Gardens and south to The Righi. Colonel Joseph Anderson, MLC (1790-1877), had served in the Peninsular War and in India, had been an early Governor of Norfolk Island, and owned a station on the Goulburn River called 'Mangalore', from his Indian days. He established himself between Punt Road and the present Anderson Street in 1845. One of his daughters married the noted Swiss-born but French-naturalised vigneron, Paul de Castella, from far up the river at Yering — Chateau Yering and St Hubert's. He was a connection of Mrs La Trobe, and brother of Hubert, who wrote the delightful *Souvenirs d'un squatter français en Australie.** Anderson was a close friend of Baron von Mueller of the Botanic Gardens, who advised his neighbours in South Yarra and Richmond on the planting of trees and laying out of gardens.

With this pleasant view of Punt Hill in front of them, no wonder many early Richmond residents chose to live on what was called River Bank. But soon this area came to be known as Cremorne and to play for a couple of decades a big role in the life of Melbourne. It was given the name of another Thames-side resort of Georgian London: the pleasure gardens of Cremorne that long vied with Ranelagh.

GEORGE COPPIN

With Cremorne comes the second of Richmond's 'big names', George Coppin, who rates a full-length biography, *Coppin the Great*, by Alex Bagot (1965). There is also a novel about Coppin and Cremorne for children, and their parents, by the late Marie Buesst, called *The Craigs of Collins Street.*

Coppin was an Englishman, of a long line of Norfolk clergy, but his father and mother were actors and he himself learned his art in Dublin at the 'old' Abbey Theatre, somewhat more extravagant and less highbrow than its successor, built up by Yeats, Synge and Lady Gregory. Coppin was in fact a superb entrepreneur in many fields and

---

*Since the above was written a translation, *Notes of an Australian Vine Grower*, has been made, with preface and notes, by C. B. Thornton-Smith (The Mast Gully Press, 1979).

a man who in his day commanded much admiration and affection.

He bought Cremorne in 1856, a huge area. Part of it had been known as Wright's Swamp and it seems to have been a billabong of the Yarra, which later was straightened and widened right up to Richmond (1891). Wright's Swamp became Cremorne Gardens, with its pier over the river for the steamers. Coppin drained the swamp into a lake and launched on it the first white swans of Australia. It was about thirty years before that the first black swans had been noted by the explorers of Western Australia and had given the name to Perth's river. There is a legend that Swan Street, Richmond, got its name from the birds. In fact, the name came from the early Swan Hotel of 1850. Perhaps it was there that the genial Coppin got his inspiration to import white swans.

There was soon to be a theatre at Cremorne, the 'Pantheon'. Coppin had for ten years been active at the 'Queen's Theatre' in Queen Street, Melbourne. The 'Queen's' was a 'real' theatre, and the old building survived, in one form or another, till about 1925. I can remember its demolition and the general surprise at the realisation that it had once been a popular theatre.

Its heyday had been in 1855 when Coppin presented Melbourne's first season of Italian opera. The leading soprano was Mme Carandini, a Tasmanian girl who had married an Italian count-in-exile with a talent for music. This they passed on to their daughter, Rosina Carandini, who later, as Mrs Palmer, sang indomitably in the Scots Church choir until a far-advanced age.

The season lasted three months and presented some fine operas: Donizetti's 'Lucrezia Borgia' and 'Lucia di Lammermoor', Bellini's 'Sonnambula', Flotow's 'Martha' and later the two very popular Irish operas, Michael Balfe's 'The Bohemian Girl' and Vincent Wallace's 'Maritana' which, like Mme Carandini, is said to have issued from Hobart.

Coppin lived for ten years in the grounds of Cremorne. During this time he served as Richmond's second Mayor, and also in the Victorian Parliament. Then he went abroad taking his Australian theatre company to America where they had a very successful tour. Meanwhile, with a growing family, he had decided to leave Cremorne and move up on to Richmond Hill. First he went to Church Street, near St Stephen's, but then he moved west across the hilltop to Lennox Street and bought 'Pine Grove'.

This was in 1866. Coppin's friend and successor as Mayor of Richmond, Joseph Bosisto, on the afternoon of his return, staged a procession of the City Fathers and several hundred citizens who, accompanied by bands and the Fire Brigade, marched up to 'Pine Grove'. The stage management was much after Coppin's heart, almost rivalling his pantomimes, balloon ascents and fireworks at Cremorne. They presented Coppin with a manifesto under the seal of Richmond:

> Sensible of your strong attachment and long service to the Borough we cannot allow you to land without expressing our pleasure at your reutrn.

It worked. That night Bosisto persuaded Coppin to return to Parliament, not the Council as previously, but this time to the Assembly as Member of Parliament for Jolimont, and later on, East Melbourne. This was a parliamentary career which, along with his other, theatrical, career, lasted for three more decades. He was generally, but not always, for he dearly loved a *coup de theatre,* even in Parliament, a Conservative — but he was always pro-Federation, and lived well into the twentieth century to see it at work.

Cremorne fell on evil days, and was subdivided in 1885. For a time Coppin's house at Cremorne became a private lunatic asylum and between 1863 and 1884 was directed by James Harcourt from Birmingham, a pioneer of evangelical social reform, who was MLA for Richmond for six years around 1870. Later a jam factory was set up, close to Cremorne but probably not on it, using Bosisto's old emblem of the rosella parrot, and rich aromas of tomato sauce and other goodies still float across the river to South Yarra and, on days of high north wind, can be smelt even on the far side of Punt Hill in Toorak Road.

Meanwhile, Coppin extravagantly enlarged Dr Black's spacious house to make it the show-place of Richmond. Then he created conservatories, aviaries, ferneries, fountains, flower gardens, sweeping lawns, with horse paddocks and stables at the rear. In most of this he was greatly helped with the advice of his friend von Mueller. I never saw 'Pine Grove' in Coppin's day, but as a boy I often roamed its gardens, still with a fairytale quality, although no longer well-kept. After Coppin's death it became a private hospital where my father as a doctor often sent patients, and I never minded how long I had to wait for him to emerge.

While Coppin lived it remained the scene of charity fêtes, of entertainment of different kinds to welcome leading actors to Melbourne. For forty years, between 1866 and 1906, the stars all came out to 'Pine Grove': Adelaide Ristori, Sarah Bernhardt, Melba, along with the great orchestras who came for the Exhibitions: Sir Charles Hallé, Sir Frederick Cowan, who was imported at a fee of £5000.

There was also much more personal entertainment, for Coppin and his wife were very hospitable and there were frequent birthday parties, dinners and dances, and wedding receptions in the big ballroom. They had numerous daughters. Constance married the son of Coppin's colleague in the Legislative Assembly and Council, Robert Stirling-Anderson from Coleraine, Co Derry. Anderson, a graduate of Trinity College, Dublin, and a Dublin lawyer, served in many Victorian Ministries.

Coppin is still remembered at Sorrento, which he helped to create, and at Coppin Avenue in Rushall Park, North Fitzroy, the Old Colonists' Association (1870), another of his inspirations. He also founded the hostel 'Gordon House' at the east end of Little Bourke Street which, after a long decay, has been elaborately recycled and its courtyards and balconies set with lawns and flowers. Shops and restaurants have replaced the old lodgings and open-air meals are served under the giant palm-tree which Coppin planted in 1894.

We have seen that Richmond came late to city status: Fitzroy, Hotham (North Melbourne) and Emerald Hill (South Melbourne) grew up much more quickly, with splendid Victorian palazzos as their Town Halls, generally set in a kind of plaza. Other inner suburbs — Carlton, Jolimont, Parkville — never became separate municipalities. 'Garryowen' complained that 'Richmond's local government was very careless' and that when the Town Hall came it was 'the right thing in the wrong place'.

The Town Hall dates from the late 'sixties, although it was planned several years earlier while Joseph Bosisto was Mayor. It was on the grand scale, dark brown brick with a tall campanile. The clock was given by Bosisto. It should have been on one of the line of Richmond hills, from

Church Street, Waltham Street, Lennox Street to Erin Street. Instead, it was badly sited down on the eastern flat.

There was a very large population influx around this time. A rough census of 1850 had claimed that half of the 9000 inhabitants were English, nearly all of them either Church of England, though a surprising proportion were 'Church of Ireland', or else Wesleyan Methodists mainly from Ireland. One-quarter were from Ireland and Catholic. Only one-sixth were Presbyterian from Scotland and Northern Ireland. The balance was changed considerably from the mid-'fifties on.

To accommodate the newcomers, the subdivisions increased at a great rate, with new streets, many with an accompanying 'Little' Street of the same name, lanes, terraces and many mere culs-de-sac. There was little of the town planning evident in Carlton, South Melbourne and North Melbourne, with their fine squares and very wide streets, such as Lincoln Square, Argyle Square, MacArthur Place and Hoddle's St Vincent's Place. But many of the narrow old streets, with a remarkable variety of architecture and occasionally a fine terrace, or two-storied houses of blue-stone or Hawthorn brick set in a large, well-tilled garden, are of rewarding interest, especially The Crofts, Rotherwood Street and Elm Grove, all south of Bridge Road, and Bowen and Highett Streets, north of Bridge Road.

We have seen that Docker named many of the first streets; Docker and Clifton, and Gipps Street linking them, are all three fine wide streets. Bosisto as Mayor and MP for twenty years, named or inspired Bosisto Street, Eucalyptus Street, and also Eliza Street, after his wife's favourite niece, a pardonable piece of nepotism, so very small was the street.

The Henty family, from Sussex, also had a share in the

christenings. Lennox Street has been attributed to the fact that it was the surname of the Dukes of Richmond, and Goodwood Street was named after their house and race-course in Sussex. Arundel Street was another Sussex name. Lennox Street, however, was a compliment to the great bridge builder David Lennox, who built the first Prince's Bridge in 1844, the single arch which then sufficed for what the American poet Karl Shapiro has called 'the toy Yarra'. The bridge builder may indeed have been of the same family.

CHURCH STREET

It would be tedious to try to cover the many Richmond streets. Richmond Hill is the most interesting area from the historical point of view, and most of the interest is still to be found in or near Church Street.

In 1861, at the entrance to Richmond, on the corner of Punt and Bridge Roads, were the larger houses, sometimes stretching back to Erin Street, of the legislators Highett, also a large landowner at Moorabbin; Hull, who soon replaced his 'Swiss Thatched Cottage' with a stone mansion; Robert Harper, a Flinders Lane magnate; Captain Octavius Burton; and Mr Joseph Walker of the Richmond National School. Walker's boys soon seized on the lines of W. S. Gilbert about the wicked Sir Despard Murgatroyd after his reformation and applied them to their headmaster.

> I've given up all my wild proceedings,
> My taste for a wandering life is waning,
> A moderate livelihood I'm gaining.
> In fact we rule a National School.

The duties are dull but I'm not complaining,
This sort of thing takes a deal of training.

There was also in Bridge Road the house of Captain Robert Wigmore, foreshadowing 'Mrs Wigg's' academy for young ladies, 'East Leigh'.

For some reason the 1862 directory extends Richmond and Church Street as far as the Yarra at Studley Park Bridge, to the far west, and includes the house of the first Speaker of the Assembly, Sir Francis Murphy, a former colonial surgeon.

Other early Richmond residents were William Nicholson, twice Premier in the 'sixties, in Rowena Parade; and W. A. F. Mitchell, President of the Legislative Council, in Darlington Parade. Sir William Mitchell (1811-84) was the son of an English vicar. He became Chief Commissioner of Police and built up the understaffed force of gold rush Victoria from seven hundred to two thousand in one year. He also performed an urgent essential service in reorganising the Melbourne police force. His home, 'Barford', was at Kyneton, but he kept up a town house just off Church Street from 1863. Three of his Mitchell granddaughters have become noted novelists.

James Francis, a Chief Secretary of Victoria, was MP for Richmond from 1859 to 1874, but seems generally to have lived elsewhere. Like Peter Lalor, he declined a knighthood — three times.

If you walk up Church Street on the eastern side from Bridge Road you would pass on the east side the Richmond Free Dispensary, set up in 1868 by Mayor Bosisto, with his predecessor George Coppin and his successor Dr Cornelius Stewart. This early clinic celebrated its centenary in 1968, with Sir Robert Menzies, Sir MacFarlane Burnet, Dr Jim Cairns, MP, and Mr Standish Keon, a former MP, playing leading roles. Like Dr Singleton's Hospital set up in Collingwood in 1869, it did a good deal to relieve the Melbourne Hospital of its overwhelming burden of out-patients.

You would also pass on the west side the very substantial Wesleyan Chapel of Gothic bluestone built in 1854 under the patronage of the first Mayor, Henry Miller, with an elegant two-storied parsonage and a large hall at its sides. The first minister bore the proud name of James de Quetteville Robin, and he has left many outstanding descendants, including Gordon Robin of Antarctic expeditions, the president of the Australian National Line, and Anglican clergy and headmasters.

One of the early ministers was the Rev. Henry Ham, whose family were to play a big role in many different fields. Most notable was Cornelius Ham, an early Lord Mayor of Melbourne, who lived next door to Coppin in Lennox Street. Another, in 1966, was appointed to the chair of radiotherapy in the great Dutch university of Utrecht.

PETER LALOR

Opposite you will still find the handsome house of Peter Lalor, a century old, but overshadowed by large new blocks of flats. There have often been protests to the Richmond Council over the Lalor house, countered by arguments that there are 'so many Lalor houses', and that he lived all over the place. Certainly, for the tense months after Eureka, very few people indeed knew where Lalor lived despite a price of £200 on his head. The loyalty of his countrymen has an echo of the long months after Culloden when Prince Charles Edward lay hidden in the Highlands with a very heavy price on his head, but no one gave him away.

Lalor is one of the great names of Richmond, almost too well-known for me to try to add anything more. Much of the fiery 'stirring' attributed to Lalor is now seen to have come from his lieutenant, the red-haired young Tuscan from Urbino, Raffaello Carboni, long referred to by historians as Carboni Rafaele, generally described as a 'Roman'.

When President Saragat of Italy was on his state visit to Australia, in 1967, one of the first requests he made on arrival was for a book on the life and writings of Carboni. He was staying at the Southern Cross, and I, as Australian ambassador to Italy accompanying him, was relieved to find that there was just such a book at one of the bookshops on that Bourke Street Hill of Content. It was in English, but that was all right because, although he did not speak English, President Saragat could read it fluently.

My grandmother could recall Patrick Lalor, the father of Peter, as a substantial farmer of 'Tenakill' in Queen's County, now Co Leix, Lalors' land for centuries, and also as a Member of the House of Commons, in her childhood. The name, she insisted, was Lalor (Law) not Lalor (Lay) as many call it nowadays. My grandfather often told of Patrick's eldest son, Fintan, a graduate of Trinity College, Dublin, where he was a contemporary and friend of his own elder brother Miles. He became a well-known economist, a member of the 'Young Ireland' movement, and was briefly imprisoned during the armed uprising of 1848. Fintan Lalor had tried to get his youngest brother Peter, then twenty-two, to join him, but Peter wrote, 'from what I have seen of the mode of conducting politics in Ireland I have had no inclination to mix myself up in them'. Peter too was to have gone up to Trinity but instead he was trained as a civil engineer. After the famine of 1848 and with the discovery of gold in Australia, Peter Lalor came to Melbourne in 1852 and then went to the diggings at Ballarat — the Eureka lead.

After the tragedy of the Eureka Stockade in November 1854 Lalor was hidden near Geelong by the family of his fiancee, Alicia Dunne, also neighbours from central Ireland. The price on his head was soon revoked and in April 1855 a Melbourne jury found the thirteen diggers charged with high treason 'not guilty'.

A year after Eureka Lalor was elected MLC. Later he became MLA and in 1880 Speaker. Although he declined the customary knighthood, Lalor was no republican. He was a traditional Speaker, maintaining great dignity and impartiality.

His great height (noted by Sir Ernest Scott in his *Short History* but abbreviated in one recent history to five feet one) had been one reason for his emerging as leader, or nominal leader, at Eureka. The loss of his left arm, and the cloak slung over his shoulder, gave him added panache. My grandmother told me he was a very tall man, 'like most men from our part of Ireland'. The proclamation shows him to have been 'five feet eleven and three-quarter inches'.

After his wife's death he gave up his big town house in Church Street and went to live across the street with his only son, Dr Joseph Lalor. He was visited there by Julian Thomas, 'The Vagabond', a few days before his death in the summer of 1889.

He had received the last rites of his church from the

priest of St Ignatius' next door, and was calmly awaiting his end — sitting in an armchair at the study window looking out over pleasant South Yarra and Toorak, courteous and gracious in his greeting, not looking like one of those who are morituri.

I remember very clearly his son, Dr Joseph Lalor, long a close friend and neighbour of my father, and a man of great courtesy, kindness and Irish charm. His son, Peter Lalor, as a medical student, often came to our house. Another son, Joe, or Joseph Peter, went to Gallipoli in 1915 and was killed. During World War II Canberra asked the High Commissioner in London, S. M. Bruce, to approach the Turkish Government and try to recover a sword worn by Peter Lalor at Eureka, and also, it seemed, carried by Joseph Peter Lalor at the Gallipoli landing.

Bruce, himself a veteran of Gallipoli and twice wounded there, from the outset of his seven years as Prime Minister in the 1920s had worked hard to establish Australian-Turkish friendship between the chivalrous enemies. Later he had been chosen to chair the important conference at Montreux in 1936 on the future of the Dardanelles and Bosphorus Straits and, both before and since, had maintained close personal relations with Ataturk and his successors, their Foreign Ministers, and a series of Turkish ambassadors in London, including an admiral and a general. As High Commissioner in London, he worked very hard throughout the war to keep Turkey neutral, and prevent the Germans from bursting through the north to join up with Rommel in North Africa.

The Turkish ambassador was delighted by the enquiry and at once guaranteed that a search be made of every war museum in Turkey for Peter Lalor's sword, and together they sat down and drafted a telegram in French, which later in the day, as Australian liaison officer with the British Foreign Office, I took to them for onward transmission to Ankara.

The summit of Church Street hill housed in the first half-century of Richmond a large number of professional men in two-storeyed buildings. The houses were in a variety of styles, many of them handsome. At 'Stonehenge' on Richmond Hill lived Alfred B. Malleson, the founder of one of the most famous of Australian firms of solicitors, now called only by his name (although among the partners were much better-known names including that of Stawell, the son of a celebrated Chief Justice, another Dublin man). Today there are no Mallesons in the directories. His name lives on in a small street in Burnley, and in the mountains where, beyond Healesville, on Mt Toolebewong, you can still see Malleson's Lookout and Malleson's Gully. A very private man, little is known of him, although his brother was a partner in one of the most famous firms of solicitors in London, 'Markby's'. He himself practised at Castlemaine and Ballarat before coming to Melbourne.

The name of Moule, of another famous firm of solicitors, is also to be found in early Church Street, and another solicitor who lived here in later years was G. F. A. Jones, who was, I think, the last non-Labor Mayor of Richmond, about 1920. The present president of the Richmond and Burnley Historical Society, Mr Laurie Lestrange, represents a third generation of the firm of Lestrange and Kennedy, in Bridge Road.

JAMES L. PURVES

Next door to Malleson you find the town house of James L. Purves, still in his early twenties, practising at Temple Court in Chancery Lane and soon to become the greatest of Victorian advocates. Certainly he was the most colourful and legendary in the history of the Bar. His father had been a pioneer landowner of south central Victoria, a man of the Scottish border. He himself had been trained in England at Trinity College Cambridge and Lincoln's Inn.

I can just remember him, and my father, for whom Mr Purves had been a hero since his boyhood, introducing me to him, later stressing this was something I should always remember. And I do, for not only was he of striking appearance, with broad brow and a wave of snow-white hair, but there was no trace in his greeting of the 'well, well, my little man' approach dear to many elderly Victorians and Edwardians. At that age, children are not as often taken in as they are perhaps a little later on. I can recognise the general accuracy of the portrait of Purves which Philip Jacobs, a barrister of the next generation, has left.

> What a splendid presence he had! And what personality! There was something magnetic about him. His rich sonorous voice, so full of expression; his daredevil manner; his insight into character; his keen and trenchant humour.

The legal firm of Purves and Purves has carried on his name. The recent death of his grandson, J. R. W. Purves, will be widely regretted. Bill Purves was scholar, musician, sportsman in many fields, including cricket and golf, a lawyer specialising in racing law, a soldier in New Guinea during World War II, and a famous, internationally-known, philatelist.

SIR WILLIAM IRVINE

The former Liberal Party leader, Chief Justice of Victoria, and for three years acting Governor of the State, Sir William Irvine, had an early link with Richmond. He came from the Co Down, and was at Trinity College, Dublin, when his father's linen mills failed and his father died. Irvine's mother was a remarkable woman, a daughter of the manse and sister of John Mitchel, of *The Nation* and 'Young Ireland' and, later, *Jail Journal*. Mitchel was convicted of treason and felony and transported to Tasmania 'for fourteen years' but, as a ticket-of-leave man, escaped and later became a famous journalist in America. William Irvine was himself a strong Unionist and very conservative, but he was immensely proud of his rebel uncle, one of the not-infrequent paradoxes of Ireland. It was the widowed Mrs Irvine who took her young family to Australia. She established them somewhere in Richmond, and her son wrote back to Ireland that he was pleased with their new environment.

Mr J. M. Bennett, of Sydney, in a recent article in the *Journal of the Royal Historical Society of Victoria,* gives a picture of life in Richmond around 1880:

> The people here, those that have come out, are very pleasant and kindly, and I suppose you have heard how much we have been asked out to tea.
>
> They drop in here at all hours from 10 am to 10 pm without much formality.

The young colonials are a poor set, physically and morally — very thin and very 'cheeky'. Their sisters have the advantage of them. They, the girls, are generally tall and buxom, with fine figures and beautifully clear complexions. But our friends who have come out from home or who are old diggers are very kind and very agreeable.

They mostly have the corners rubbed off them by their intercourse with so many different kinds of people. Every man here knows everybody else; which is more the result of habit with the old colonials than anything else.

Although he was known as 'Iceberg Irvine' there was warmth beneath the ice. Lady Bassett has written that 'though he was punctilious he did not at heart cease to be natural. He was both courteous and kind'.

Mr Bennett also states that the family migrated centuries ago from Spain to Ireland. He mentions that, at Trinity, he won a valuable prize for Italian; but, if he had Latin blood, it was probably more Spanish than Italian. Once as a Chief Justice he had to try a complicated case of copyright in a valuable edition of the works of Cervantes. An over-eager barrister assured him early on that an interpreter would be provided for translation. I shall never forget the annoyance quickly submerged in polite hauteur of the Chief Justice's reply: 'That will not be necessary'.

The doctors in this 'salubrious' area were very numerous. Dr Wm. Gregory, Dr Thomas Stillman and Dr Cornelius Stewart were all surgeons. Stewart was the fourth Mayor of Richmond.

A few years ago, when I was stationed in Italy, I often

met an English resident of Florence who had played an active role in 'intelligence' during the war and since then had settled in a comfortable villa which had one of the finest private libraries I have ever seen. He asked me if I had ever heard of his maternal grandfather named Stewart, a pioneer surgeon of Melbourne, of whom he knew little and from whose estate his private income was derived, and it seemed pretty clear that the grandfather was this pioneer settler on Richmond Hill.

Later came William Graham, MD, of London, full of stories of his relative General Graham, of Balgowan, later Lord Lynedoch, in the Peninsular War and the victor of Barossa, commemorated in South Australia's wine valley. He married the daughter of another Richmond Mayor, John Adam, of Lennox Street, who, with his public-spirited family, was among the real heroes of the bursting of the boom. Other doctors on Richmond Hill were Mr Florence O'Sullivan, Dr Duigan, Dr Joseph Lalor, and Dr Peter Reid.

One of the most interesting doctors of Richmond was Frederick Elsner, born in Dublin in 1856 and trained at the Rotunda Hospital. His family were probably German refugees of 1848, and he was himself a German scholar. There is a legend that he was nearly related to Joseph Elsner, one of the great names in Polish music, a German from Silesia who became director of the Warsaw Opera and Conservatorium. He was the teacher of Chopin but soon detected a genius and wisely decided: 'Leave Chopin alone; his is an uncommon way because his gifts are uncommon.'

Coming to Victoria in 1885, Frederick Elsner began practice in Richmond and gradually moved up Church Street hill from 'Richmond Villa', No. 189, first to 201, then to 319, and finally to 359, which is still standing. My father took it over from Dr Elsner for a few years in the mid-'nineties.

He was the first Melbourne dermatologist, and was appointed to the Alfred Hospital in 1886. His story has been fully told by one of his successors of nearly a century later, Dr W. J. Jamieson, in his short book *The Genesis of Melbourne Dermatology*.* Six years later Elsner moved on to Sydney, and Dr Jamieson has traced his romantic story to his premature death at Moree, New South Wales, 'of heat apoplexy on a day of 40°C'.

THE MONASH FAMILY

The top of the hill was not confined to doctors and lawyers. There was the family of W. B. Burnley, of the original 'block' of 1839, by now vastly increased in wealth. One of his descendants, Mrs J. M. McMillan, is vice-president of the Richmond Historical Society. There was, on the corner of Church and Catherine Streets, Louis Monash, from Germany, the father of the great general. Louis Monash went there in the late 'sixties. His son John had been born in June 1865. Louis Monash was of a Polish Jewish family, long established in what was then Prussia. He came to Australia at twenty-one, in the gold rush of 1853, and founded a softgoods firm, importing from Germany. He lived briefly in West Melbourne where his children were born. Settling in Richmond, he sent his son to St Stephen's school for boys, on to the Government School, and then to the Scotch College on Eastern Hill. The Monash family were all tri-lingual, in English, German and French, and John Monash went on to Melbourne University to become a

*Australian Medical Publishing Co Ltd, Sydney, 1974.

Renaissance-type man in his equipment, with high degrees in arts, law and engineering.

Catherine Street has long since become Elm Grove, and its elms have been replaced by a splendid hillside avenue of planes. Just around the corner, at No. 3 Elm Grove, there is a house of three or two and a half storeys, with a curious ecclesiastical look which still intrigues historical researchers. It is said that there are crosses on the gables, the remains of a chapel, a stained-glass window, and an unusual fireplace adapted from an altar. The architect is said to have been Wardell, who designed St Ignatius' church nearby, and it seems that one owner was a vicar of St Stephen's. Part of it dates from 1845. For many years early this century it was the house of a well-known journalist, of Irish and French stock, Pierre Bellew. His son Peter more recently represented Australia in Paris on the staff of UNESCO.

Another French link was the house on the southern slope of Church Street, occupied by a French Consul of the early 'sixties, Adolphe Truiy.

THE VAUCLUSE : THE RYAN FAMILY

Perhaps the most romantic-sounding name in Richmond, a French one, is 'the Vaucluse', a private street (rare in our city) which once was periodically closed by gates at either end. It rambles in curves from the west side of Church Street hill back to Rowena Parade, the narrow street which descends all the way to Punt Road. Its northern side has been for just under a century the Vaucluse Convent and it is hard to see over the high wall. But along with the convent buildings of red brick there is a splendid old bluestone mansion much older than the rest. As a first guess, someone who knew their Petrarch, or the lovely Provençal valley with its fountain in the foothills of the Alps, the 'closed valley', must have given the place its name.

It was once thickly lined with oaks and elms, and still has the look of a country lane. The south side of Vaucluse is a row of Victorian houses, late and early. This land belonged to a young overlander, a grazier merchant called Daniel Campbell, the second Member of Parliament for Richmond. Along with William Highett, MP, in Erin Street, he was one of the earliest members of the Melbourne Club, founded in 1838. In 1856, when he was forty, he bought this long stretch of land and during the next ten years built a large wooden house of two storeys. (Vaucluse first appears in the Richmond Directory in 1865.) Campbell probably gave it the name because he had owned land near Vaucluse Bay in Sydney close to the famous Vaucluse House of William Wentworth. It was not Wentworth who named it but, probably, Sir Henry Brown Hayes, a Knight and former Sheriff of Cork, transported for trying to abduct and marry the Quaker heiress Miss Mary Pike, a Ward of Chancery. He may have had the story of Petrarch and his lost love, Laura, of Vaucluse, in mind. Another part of 'Campbell's house' was a single-storeyed villa of simple lines with an arched door and a fanlight above it edged with French ruby glass which once had a coat of arms: a snake twined around a stick and the motto *Audax et Prudens*.

Campbell lived up to the first part of the motto but not the second. He spent extravagantly, soon had to mortgage his house and his estate, selling it to the Christian Brothers in 1875. They turned it into a school. A Gothic tower, 'The Tower House', rises three storeys at the back of the house, probably built by the Brothers.

The Woolcott family of lawyers were closely linked to Vaucluse. There was also Captain Septimus Martin. Another resident was James Graves, MP, an Irishman born at Maryborough in Queen's County (Co Leix), a graduate of Trinity College, Dublin, who sold his family estates in Co Wexford and arrived in Victoria in 1864 going on to lease stations in many districts. From 1877 to 1902 he was MP for Delatite, having settled at Mansfield. There is much about him and his political career in Joan Gillison's *Country Doctor*. Alfred Deakin said of Graves that he was enthusiastic for Orange principles in Protestant areas and ecumenical at Catholic meetings, a criticism sometimes heard even today when ecumenism is almost universal.

The best-known name of Vaucluse, however, is that of Charles Ryan, father and son, in the late 'sixties and 'seventies. The older Charles Ryan was from Co Kilkenny, who overlanded from New South Wales to Victoria in 1846, and took up land around Longwood, first at 'Kilfera' after his birthplace and then at 'Killeen' where most of his large family were born.

Later, from 1868 to 1873, he lived in Vaucluse, next door to Tower House, until he went up to Mt Macedon and created the famous twenty-odd acre garden of 'Derriweit Heights', with the aid of the new director of the Botanical Gardens, Guilfoyle, who had just succeeded von Mueller and was a landscape specialist.

His granddaughter, Lady Casey, in *An Australian Story,* describes him well:

A firm but gentle face and the eyes, in spite of their alertness and gleam, essentially innocent. The enthusiasm, sometimes gullibility, that runs like a streak through many of the Ryans, is here for all to see.

How true is that description of the many in Victoria, and noticeably in early Richmond, who mingle the Irish and the English blood.

The family who grew up in Vaucluse soon scattered far afield. The eldest son Charles became a leading Melbourne surgeon. As a very young man after study in Edinburgh, Bonn and Vienna, he became a surgeon in the Turkish army for nearly two years, during the Russo-Turkish War. He went through the long siege of Plevna, and wrote a book about it, *Under the Red Crescent.*

A daughter married the senior officer of the Royal Navy in Australian waters, Admiral Lord Charles Scott. Their son, Sir David Scott, was long head of the Consular department of the Foreign Office and a good friend to the infant diplomatic service of Australia. He had been born in Sydney, and once told me that, although he left it before he was three, he had only to shut his eyes to see Sydney Harbour from the angle of the lawn of Admiralty House.

Another Ryan daughter, Mrs Ellis Rowan, was one of Australia's earliest wanderers (in the tradition of Scotland's Isabella Bird of *Unbeaten Tracks in Japan,* and many great Englishwomen since then). She was widowed very young, and for many years travelled the world, first New Zealand, then America, the West Indies, New Guinea and all over Australia, solitary and fearless. She painted a huge series of the wildflowers and birds of Australia and New Guinea. They were bought by the Commonwealth Government and a number of them hang in Australian official houses all over the world.

Miss Mary Turner Shaw, in her classic *Builders of Melbourne*, a history of the many generations of the Cockram family, made an observation which struck me as highly significant:

> Every family has — or should have (just such) an Auntie Liz. . . . The value of the information they have to hand down is often underrated until it is too late. Auntie Liz Cockram remembered everything, in fragments . . . confirming the accuracy of family legends.

To just such an Auntie Liz I owe my interest, such as it is, in early Richmond. Charming, generous and kind, sympathetic but always astringent, she maintained links with her mother's family by visits to Ireland, and narrowly escaped being made an absentee landlord. Unfortunately, or perhaps wisely, she wrote little or nothing. She married, very young, Alfred Colton, son of the then Premier of South Australia, and went to Adelaide, becoming immersed in the affairs of an active political family. Her stories were only in vivid flashes, all by word of mouth, on her too rare visits to Melbourne.

I remember particularly her descriptions of Vaucluse and especially Mrs Rowan, when briefly Mrs Rowan came home from her wanderings. My aunt was clearly one of those who were under the spell of this amazing woman. 'As a schoolgirl I used to go around the corner from "Clifton" to the Vaucluse whenever I could, and literally sit at her feet while she painted . . . and talked.'

In the next generation this Ryan family has sent its children all over the world. Lady Casey's career and many talents are known to everyone, and I will only add that her book, *Early Melbourne Architecture,* is one of the great stimuli to preserving and recording the first century.

Less known, perhaps, at the moment, is her brother, Colonel Rupert Ryan. From Harrow and Woolwich, where he passed out top, he went into British Army and served in the Middle East and in France, with DSO and many other decorations. He then became Deputy Allied High Commissioner for the Rhineland, and, in fact, the High Commissioner, serving for several years in this post, at which his sister Maie, later Lady Casey, both being then unmarried, was his hostess. Later he had long experience of Thailand and of Russia, speaking the languages. Then he returned to Australia and in 1940 became MP for Flinders, long the seat of S. M. Bruce, which he held until his sudden untimely death in 1952.

It was no mean achievement to fit so rapidly and well into political life in Australia from which he had been absent for over thirty years. His contributions to the rare debates on foreign affairs in the 'thirties, 'forties and 'fifties were always thorough, wise and witty, and the infant Australian Foreign Affairs Service should remember gratefully his interventions in its defence.

BURNLEY

The eastern slopes of Richmond Hill ran down to the flats where the main street was known as Burnley, after the pioneer, W. B. Burnley, and soon the whole area was called after him. It was much subdivided and from the 'seventies on had many new factories. One of the earliest was George Fincham's, the famous organ builder. It was the early home of Bedggood's Richmond Boot Factory. Bryant and May's, of the matches, started in Burnley. The Wertheim Piano

Factory in Bendigo Street later became, in 1942, the factory of H. J. Heinz, until in 1955 they moved to Dandenong and was replaced by Channel 9. H. U. Alcock and Co built billiard tables and their fame spread far. By 1880 they had exported a magnificent table of mulga wood for the King of Hawaii's Iolani Palace — still to be seen in Honolulu.

The rather forgotten district of 'Yarraberg' lay between Burnley Street and River Street — the reach of the Yarra looking on to St James's Park. The most famous product of Burnley was neither its great organs nor its pianos — it was the voice of Melba.

DAVID MITCHELL : DAME NELLIE MELBA

Her father David Mitchell could also claim to be one of the great names of Richmond. He was a Scot, born in Angus, the son of a farmer, and apprenticed as a mason. Still young, barely twenty-three, he arrived in 1852 and founded the Burnley Street brickworks, and before long had a vast industry at Lilydale, and large farms and vineyards along the Upper Yarra. He lived near his factory, building his 'Doonside', a tall house of stucco on brick with a low yellow tower, and his home for the next thirty years. He built the Scots Church and for years sang in its choir, as did his daughter, though she alternated with St Francis's in Lonsdale Street. My father used to tell rather proudly that David Mitchell had invited him, an undergraduate of sixteen, to go up with him in the 'last lift' to the top of the Scots Church spire.

Under various architects, he built for half the Scots of Melbourne; Menzies Hotel, Paterson Laing & Bruce's vast headquarters in Flinders, whence a young Prime Minister was to emerge, the Exhibition Building with its great dome, the Presbyterian Ladies' College in East Melbourne, where his daughter went as a day girl in 1876, the Richmond Town Hall, where Melba made her debut at the age of eight or six. The dates vary a little as is legitimate for great opera singers. More than any other she battled with Time and won.

Some say her debut was at the old Lennox Street Congregational Church. Her first contribution was her father's favourite 'Comin' thro' the Rye' which, with 'Home, Sweet Home', Tosti's 'Goodbye' and her matchless 'Addio' from *La Bohème,* remained in her repertoire all her life.

I like her own story of her first school in Richmond, Mrs Wigmore's 'East Leigh'. My Aunt Liz, her contemporary there, confirmed the story of the boarders having to take a cold shower every morning at six, and Helen Mitchell's ingenious theatrical device of going under the shower, with an umbrella held over her head, while the splashing rang through 'East Leigh'. For the Stirling girls of that generation, and their brothers, Melba was above any criticism till the end.

ST IGNATIUS

One major event in Richmond was the coming of St Ignatius' Church. In 1867 the Catholic Bishop, Dr Bede Polding, laid the foundation stone. He sent for a group of five Jesuit fathers, headed by Fr Joseph Dalton, to minister to the 4000 Catholics of Richmond. He had bought an acre and a half, on the very summit of Church Street hill, from Dr Cornelius Stewart. The plans were drawn up by William Wardell, the pupil of Pugin and architect of St Patrick's. It was of basalt bluestone, with white Sydney-stone dressing.

The stone for the spire, added after Wardell's death, came from Footscray and the Hawkesbury River.

The Gothic nave, aisle and tower were finished within ten years, the transept within another ten, in 1888. The magnificent spire, still towering over Richmond and visible for miles, is seventy metres high, the second highest in Melbourne. It was dedicated fifty years ago, at the end of 1928.

Fincham's of Richmond built the splendid organ. It was first used at the Colonial Exhibition of 1875. The first organist, Gerlach, soon gave way to a much-loved Venetian, Zelman, in 1890.

One of the many beauties of the church is St Ignatius' Chapel — commemorating also St Frances Xavier and St Francis Borgia, Duke of Gandia in Spain, the third general of the Society. It is strange to think that the family of Borgia popes in the next generation also provided a saint.

There was a little ecumenical flutter over the church bell. The old Methodist church, almost next door, had to instal a deeper-toned bell to make for harmony.

Soon much of Vaucluse was attached to the great church. Its large hall opened its doors in the summer of 1883 to two notable Irish political figures, John and William Redmond, the one not long out of Trinity College, Dublin, the other not long out of the famous Jesuit school of Clongowes Wood. John had succeeded his father and many other Redmond ancestors as MP for Wexford in the House of Commons at the age of twenty-three. They were touring the English-speaking world to represent the Land League of Parnell, and to repudiate any link between Parnell and the murders in Phoenix Park, Dublin, in the previous spring.

The lively William Redmond turned twenty-one, and was elected to the House of Commons while in Australia. Both brothers married Australians, of the Dalton family of Orange, New South Wales. Ivo Bligh's English XI was playing the first Tests in Melbourne and the Redmonds, particularly John, who had been captain of cricket at Clongowes, were often at the Cricket Ground. They were disappointed that they were not able to use the Richmond and other Town Halls, as they did in England, and had to use church or school halls.

But two distinguished Irish-Australian lawyers, both afterwards judges of the High Court, Frank Gavan Duffy and Henry Bourne Higgins, took the platform. One was a Catholic, the other was not. The Redmonds raised £15,000, after John Redmond's speech:

> Let us join for every Imperial purpose and defend the Empire which is the heritage of both of us, but let us give up once for all the attempt to rule the domestic affairs of each other.

In World War I John Redmond's only son fought with an Irish regiment in France, and William Redmond, in his late forties, was killed at Messines.

Scotland was by no means excluded from old Richmond. Next to Coppin's 'Pine Grove' there was, and still is, a small Presbyterian Church, now turned into a film studio. It had a fine Fincham organ long since transferred to Chadstone. My uncle George Stirling was for a time its organist *en titre,* a post that he, with a passion for all forms of music, combined, very ecumenically, with being for years the regular organist of St Stephen's; and his friend Fr Dalton would often invite him to play at St Ignatius. All three organs were by Fincham.

Close to the Presbyterian Church was the house of a venerable Scot named Robert Inglis, whom I visited as a child with my father. His widowed daughter, Mrs Kennedy, had lately come back from Scotland to look after him. Years before, a famous Scottish family of musicians had toured Australia. One of them had married the daughter of the then Mayor of Richmond.

Several of the Scottish-Australian Kennedys achieved fame — the violinist Daisy Kennedy, who married the pianist Benno Moisewitch (and later the dramatist John Drinkwater), her brother Laurie, and Marjory, Mrs Kennedy-Fraser, who collected and arranged most of the famous songs of the Hebrides. Another daughter married Tobias Matthay, professor of piano at the London Royal College of Music.

Close by in Lennox Street, from the 'sixties on, appears the name Samuel Burston, Maltster, a name which, unchanged in four generations, has given and continues to give immense and distinguished service to Australia as a whole in many spheres.

ERIN STREET

The western part of Richmond Hill, Erin Street — which got its name early on, in 1840 — praised by Mrs Bell for its outlook to the Plenty Ranges and served by its own little railway station, West Richmond, has had its ups and downs like the rest. The Surveyor Hoddle's great house, 'Millewa', after an interval as a Salvation Army training school, became Bethesda Hospital, and William Highett's 'Yalcowinna' became Epworth Hospital. The fine town house, 'Ben Nevis', home of two Scottish doctors in succession, Dr Donald McColl and Dr Agnew, also became a part of Epworth.

It was flanked by an even more striking house, 'Ainslie', the name of its family, also, in later generations, medical; it had an Italian mosaic verandah and a fine cedar staircase. Epworth also bought, during World War II, Bosisto's laboratory where the eucalyptus oil from his various distilleries in the Dandenongs was refined.

Hoddle also built a large town house at the corner of Bourke and Spencer Streets, 'the West End', where he spent long years of retirement till his death at nearly ninety. He enlivened them by music — he was a skilled organist — and making translations from the Spanish. After his death his much younger widow re-married and went to live at 'Millewa' in Erin Street.

(In Dr Robert Zacharin's book, lately published, called *Emigrant Eucalyptus*, on the trees sent all over the world, much is told of Bosisto's activities and how his plant produced 7600 litres a year. He also tells of 'a youthful visit to Australia — little known — in 1870 by Arthur Balfour, later Prime Minister of Great Britain, and of his collection of eucalyptus seeds which he added to the eucalypts at his family seat of Whittinghame in East Lothian, first planted there in 1858'.)

The great Dr Adam Cairns, the pioneer Presbyterian, lived in Erin Street. Sir Clive Fitts has recorded inimitably the story of this street, his own birthplace and early home, both from the architectural and medical sides. Writing of the interior of No. 39, a towered house, later shorn of its tower which had served to store trunks of papers and letters, old portraits and photographs and bric-à-brac, Clive Fitts gives an affectionate description of a Richmond town house of the late Victorian period. (He himself, born along with the Commonwealth of Australia, in the last few days of Queen

Victoria's lifetime, has lived under six reigns.) Even in the Edwardian days which he first remembers, as do I, his school-fellow at the nearby Scotch College on Eastern Hill, 'there was still gas light, chandeliers hung above heavy Victorian tables; there were coal fires, black marble fireplaces and mantelpieces and a black woollen rug to invite reading by flickering firelight. Outside lamplighters passed on bicycles and sometimes a German band played'.

Erin Street ends at the frontier of Richmond and East Melbourne, Hoddle Street, the northern extension of Punt Road, rightly called after Melbourne's talented surveyor. Its Anglicans were drawn across the frontier to Holy Trinity, close to Bishopscourt, a beautiful bluestone church, built in 1864, burnt down on New Year's Day, 1905, a Sunday; or, beyond, to St Peter's, beside St Patrick's Cathedral, the oldest church of all, with its strong Anglo-Catholic tradition. The adherents of the Church of Scotland were drawn to the Cairns Memorial Church in the heart of East Melbourne, of almost cathedral proportions, but never completed. Its manse was in Erin Street, the home of the great Dr Adam Cairns. The Scots of the area who built Cairns Memorial Church included the kindred families of Sharp, of the timber mills, and Blair, linked with *The Age*.

At the south corner of Erin and Hoddle Streets were the houses of Dr Tom Boyd and Dr William Boyd, brothers. Clive Fitts records that Dr William Boyd gained fame for discovering that the third husband of the infamous triple murderess, Mrs Martha Needle, had died from arsenical poisoning.

Ireland too has its echo in Erin Street. 'Malahide' at No. 17 was called after the old castle in Co Dublin of the Norman family of Talbots. (It was at the Dublin Malahide that the rich collection of papers of James Boswell were discovered some decades ago.) The Richmond house was the home of Frank Talbot, an entrepreneur in the Coppin tradition, who died there in 1949. He was impresario of the Australian tours of Madame Emma Calvé, the most famous of all Carmens, Dame Clara Butt and Sir Harry Lauder, Adeline Genée, Fritz Kreisler, Ruth Draper, Edna Thomas, 'the lady from New Orleans', and the Sistine Chapel Choir. He converted the old Mechanics Institute, of 1843, later the 'Athenaeum Hall', into the modern Athenaeum Theatre, opening with Barrie's *Dear Brutus* in 1924. For years it was a cinema, devoted almost wholly to high-quality British films, with brief returns to plays and intervals of darkness before reverting permanently and happily to drama with the Melbourne Theatre Company. There is a fine photographic portrait of the genial Frank Talbot by his friend and neighbour, Dr Julian Smith, in the National Gallery.*

There were also German families in Erin Street — Otto Yuncken, a draughtsman from South Australia on the staff of the great builder and worker for the Anglican Church, Clements Langford, and father of a line of distinguished architects, and Maximilian Kreitmayer, whose descendants have given much to the theatre and kindred enterprises in Melbourne. He himself set up 'The Waxworks' in central Bourke Street, the southern hemisphere's counterpart of 'Madame Tussaud's'. Here you could, in the Chamber of Horrors, see Ned Kelly, Deeming and Mrs Needle. Probably the first cinema in Melbourne was set up beside the wax-

*'Sarsfield' in Erin Street recalls another Norman family and Patrick Sarsfield, the Jacobite cavalry commander, hero of the battle of Aughrim and the siege of Limerick. Later, as Marshal of France, he was killed at Landen in the Netherlands, exclaiming as he tried to staunch a fatal wound: 'Oh, that this was for Ireland.'

works in the shape of a Pullman carriage where, after realistic train-puffing and bell-ringing, you could travel to Jamaica or Sweden.

LENNOX STREET : THE HENTY FAMILY

There remains the central section of Richmond Hill, the plateau between Lennox Street and Waltham Street. This was the domain of James Henty, the merchant prince of the pioneer family, of whom Lady Bassett has painted a full and affectionate portrait. She tells how, until his death in 1882 at an advanced age, he walked daily to his office in the city.

Returning to Australia in 1851, after three years in England, James Henty entered the Victorian Parliament and built 'Richmond Hill', described at the time as 'a house with a large garden in the straggling village of Richmond', but for many years a centre and symbol of the old Richmond. It stretched from Waltham Place to Goodwood Street. It was a quiet house, compared with say Coppin's 'Pine Grove', but it housed a large family and was very hospitable. The eldest son was called Richmond. The next, Henry, long lived next door to his father and later in Church Street. A son-in-law, James Balfour, MP, a Scot, also lived next door in Waltham Street, but they fell out and parted company professionally.

Miss Mary Henty lived at 'Richmond Hill', her birthplace, for eighty years. She was long a graceful impresario at St Stephen's, leading its large choir of men and women, the latter in grey robes and mortar boards. She married rather late in life and her only son, Arundel Henty Wilson, sold 'Richmond Hill' after her death in 1928.

It was acquired by 'Pelaco', who built the vast and ugly

shirt factory over the sites of both 'Richmond Hill' and 'Pine Grove'. A precedent had been set at the turn of the century by the building of a boot factory in the centre of nearby Jolimont, followed by the dooming of beautiful and peaceful Jolimont Square (only one of whose houses remains).

Richmond may no longer have its 'country atmosphere' — 'Garryowen's' *rus in urbe* with the 'beautiful extensive slopes on both sides, very salubrious' — but it can still stir estate agents to lyrical description. As late as ten years ago, in 1969, one such effort earned the heading from *The Age,* 'Oasis in Richmond' and the comment: 'A lively tree setting in the heart of Richmond? With due respect to historic Richmond, home of the redoubtable Tigers, it seems unlikely.'

For this authority 'the heart of Richmond' was Francis Street, a little street on the Burnley side, only a stone's throw from the Town Hall and the busy crossroads of Bridge Road and Church Street. It was called after James Francis, MP, and Chief Secretary of Victoria. 'The house, of timber, delightfully renovated, has a beautifully laid out courtyard with barbecue area . . . sunlight sets the keynote. It all adds up to an atmosphere of space and serenity away from the hustle of city life.'

Ten years later *The Age*'s real estate editor, Ray Davie, writes of a house in Richmond Terrace on what he called, not without justice, 'that rather amorphous entity "Richmond Hill" ', with its upper storey balconied above 'long views over dear jumbled old Richmond to Melbourne's cathedrals, dwarfing those earlier cathedrals, St Paul's and St Pat.'s. Look around and there's Government House; look still further and there's the famous ball on the Dimmey building. One can almost imagine the poet William Wordsworth standing here beefing out a fragment from his 'Upon Westminster Bridge':

> This city now doth like a garment, wear
> The beauty of the morning: silent, bare
> Ships, towers, domes, theatres, and temples lie
> Open unto the fields, and to the sky:
> All bright and glittering in the smokeless air.

On the other hand, perhaps not.

But let's come down from poetic heights to practicality — a good buy for someone who wants to be very close to the city, shops, transport, but doesn't want a lot of property to care for.'

Perhaps, after all, the vanished Richmond is rather illusory. I have tried, by research in some detail, to atone for the fact that I never lived there and thus have viewed it through the eyes of my father and his elder sister, and the softening distance of time. Perhaps it is better to write of old Richmond in verse, and I am indebted to Judith Baird who has allowed me to quote her poem *Richmond* (1979):

On streets which once, in leisured days, transversed
    A realm of grace and elegance,
Great juggernauts belch noxious fumes,
    Pausing impatiently as garish crimson glows,
Then, at the green roar urgently on
    To gain their pre-determined destinations.

Where once were heard the gentle evening sounds
    Of music, laughter, and erudite exchange,
Now unmelodious noise blares constantly, sans pity,
    From wired metallic boxes — rendering quite
        impossible
The almost-forgotten communication of the voice,
    And needless the art of thought.

The ghosts of Richmond — Docker, Coppin, Black —
    If they still wander down the Church Street hill,
Must view with wonder, tinged with deep dismay,
    The 'trendy' trappings of this once-familiar place;
'One B.R. unit, all mod. cons., car space at rear' —
    Where now the bush, the orchards, gardens green?

So much has gone, and cannot be regained
    Except through constant, vigilant desire
To preserve, for those who follow on,
    A clear illuminating account of times long past:
The future of that past rests not with those who
        remember,
    But with those who, remembering, faithfully record.

The old Richmond goes on. St Stephen and St Ignatius still stand guard on top of the hill, more often than not hearing musical Italian accents rather than the soft southern Irish. The scent of the gum-leaf being distilled no longer sweetens Erin Street, but it houses two great shrines of medical and surgical healing. The fine little Corinthian library in Church Street South, a supplement to the large original library at the Town Hall, has gone, but it has been replaced by a large and up-to-the-minute Richmond City library, on two levels, with art gallery and theatre.

Vaucluse has lost too many of its oaks and elms. But you can still hear in its school halls, which rang to the rich and persuasive voices of John Redmond and his brother, *The Sorcerer, Box and Cox* and other rare as well as the better-known Gilbert and Sullivan operas, splendidly presented by the Loyola Musical Society.

There are no signs of Coppin the Great's theatre of Cremorne or his hospitable dances and theatricals at 'Pine Grove', but, at the hall of the old bluestone Wesleyan Church, once a school, you can still hear, in much more comfort, the Pumpkin Players putting on the latest English and foreign successes from London.

And a little paddle-steamer with a stern-wheel, and a discotheque, will once again carry you up Melbourne's river from Prince's Bridge to Richmond.

Bibliography

Bagot, Alec: *Coppin the Great* (Melbourne, 1965).

Bassett, Marnie: *The Hentys — An Australian Colonial Tapestry* (London, 1954).

Bell, Agnes Paton: *Melbourne John Batman's Village* (Melbourne, 1965).

Bennett, J. M.: Article in *Victorian Historical Journal*, 1978, 'Notes on the Life of Sir William Irvine'.

Casey, Maie, and others: *Early Melbourne Architecture 1840-1888* (London, 1953).

Casey, Maie: *An Australian Story 1837-1907* (London, 1962).

de Castella: *Souvenirs d'un squatter français en Australie* (Paris, 1880).

Fitts, Clive: *Recollections of a Bookworm* (Melbourne, 1974).

'Garryowen' (Edmund Finn): *The Chronicles of Early Melbourne 1835 to 1852*.

Grant, James, and Serle, Geoffrey: *The Melbourne Scene 1803-1956* (Melbourne, 1978).

Jacobs, Philip: *Famous Australian Trials* (Melbourne, 1942).

Jamieson, W. J.: *The Genesis of Melbourne Dermatology, Frederick William Elsner* (Australian Medical Publishing Co, Sydney, 1974).

McCrae, Hugh: *Georgiana's Journal* (Sydney, 1934).

Moore, Brian: *St Ignatius', Richmond* (Melbourne, 1972).

Royal Historical Society of Victoria: *Victorian Historical Journal*. 1913 Volume, Gleanings from *The Australian*

(Richmond daily), 1859-1861.

— 1975 Volume, 'James Harcourt'.

Serle, Geoffrey: *The Golden Age. A history of the colony of Victoria 1851-1861.*

Serle, Geoffrey, with James Grant: *The Melbourne Scene 1803-1956* (Melbourne, 1963 and 1978).

Shaw, Mary Turner: *On Mount Emu Creek* (Melbourne, 1970).

— *Builders of Melbourne* (Melbourne, 1972).

Stirling, Alfred: *Joseph Bosisto* (Melbourne, 1970).

— *Gang Forward: A Stirling Note Book* (Melbourne, 1972).

Turner, Ian: *Peter Lalor* (Melbourne, 1974).

'Vagabond, The': (Julian Thomas) *The Vagabond Papers* (Melbourne).

Westgarth, William: *Personal Recollections of Early Melbourne, 1888.*

Zacharin, Robert: *Emigrant Eucalypts* (Melbourne, 1979).

Thanks

My thanks go to Miss Judith Baird, Mr Thomas Bostock, The Lady Casey, Sir Clive Fitts, Dr W. J. Jamieson, Mr Clive Langdon, Miss Mary Turner Shaw, and Mrs Harold White, for the use of their wide research; Miss Patricia Reynolds and staff members of the La Trobe Library, the Royal Historical Society of Victoria, and the Richmond and Burnley Historical Society, and, for her help with the index, Mrs J. Bielicki; and my sister Miss Dorothy Stirling, generally.

Index